AF687207

THE

INTELLIGENCE

WE BUILT

A Journey into Artificial Intelligence and Human Ingenuity

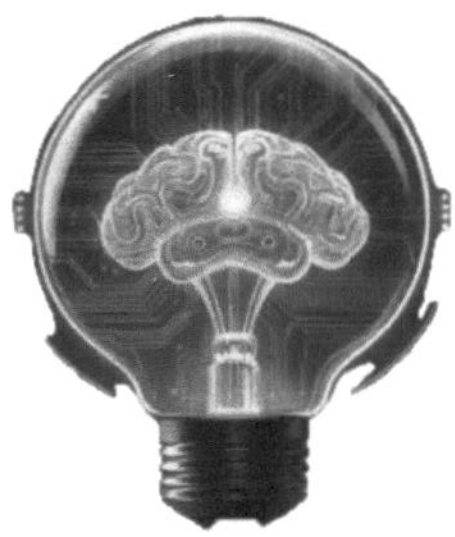

Steven Jones

COPYRIGHT PAGE

Copyright © 2026 by Steven Jones

All right reserved

No part of this book may be reproduced in any form or by any electronic or mechanical means, including information storage and retrieval systems, without written permission from the author, except for the use of brief quotation in a book review.

Table of Contents

PREFACE

I did not set out to write a book about artificial intelligence.

As with so many people who work closely with technology, I've been surrounded by it for some time. It started as a tool; a method to accomplish something useful; a model that made forecasts better; a system that sorted through information more efficiently; a dashboard that helped to give decision-makers a feeling of less uncertainty. At no point was there a dramatic realization that something profoundly new was occurring. It was more subtle than that. As time went on, the systems merely got better. They were more dependable. More accessible.

At some point, however, I began to notice a change. It wasn't simply in what computers could do, but in how people thought about them. Conversations had changed how decisions were made, and that felt different. Questions that had previously taken hours or days to resolve through lengthy discussion were resolved in seconds by predictive models. While the answers provided by these predictive models were often impressive, they were also defining how judgment was exercised.

That transformation has stuck with me.

There are two common ways in which artificial intelligence is typically framed in public discourse. One frames AI as a revolution that will dramatically alter nearly all aspects of life. The other views it as a potential menace that must be contained before it spirals completely out of control. Both of these approaches fail to capture a crucial reality. The majority of AI's impact is mundane. It occurs in everyday decisions. In obvious suggestions. In options that appear prominently at the top of screens. In predictions that seem reasonable. AI operates behind the scenes and usually doesn't draw attention to itself. Because of that, it's easy to overlook the fact that it is a designed entity.

This book arose out of an increasingly persistent unease. An unease that we were rapidly advancing toward creating certain technologies without stopping to think about what we were building and why. Not whether the technology works. Clearly, it does. But why are we designing it the way we are? What presumptions lead to the way it is designed? What compromises do we quietly accept, and what does it mean when intelligence – an attribute we have always associated with human experience – starts to exist outside of us?

The more deeply I dug into the subject matter, the clearer it became to me that artificial intelligence isn't simply a story about machines. It's a story about people. Our unwillingness to accept limits. We need to make uncertainty manageable. Our conviction is that if something can be quantified, it can be improved.

There is merit in that conviction. There is innovation. There is genius.

And there is risk.

I have written this book neither as an engineer explaining his code, nor as a detractor forewarning of catastrophic collapse. Rather, I wrote it as someone who has witnessed intelligent systems evolve from theory to application. I have observed the enthusiasm in research laboratories. I have seen the urgency in boardrooms. I have seen the reticence in policy-making circles. I have seen the growing dependence that emerges when a system demonstrates value.

Artificial intelligence didn't occur by happenstance. It represents the culmination of decades of curiosity and tenacity. It evidences our ingenuity. However, it also represents our values, often more explicitly than we might anticipate.

If this book serves as anything, I hope it encourages readers to pause, not to reject progress or uncritically celebrate it, but to examine it critically. To view artificial intelligence not as remote or abstract, but as an integral part of our daily experiences. As something created by human choice. As something that is currently being defined.

We have created this intelligence. Examining it may be one of the most genuine ways to examine ourselves.

INTRODUCTION

The first formal meeting for AI was held in 1956 at Dartmouth College. This was a very early time in computing history; computers took up entire rooms, memory was measured in kilobytes, and processing power was both fragile and extremely expensive. At the same time, there was a great deal of optimism; if reasoning and learning could be represented in mathematical terms, then intelligence may not be a mysterious phenomenon. It may be possible to represent it computationally.

For many decades, however, progress in developing AI was spotty. Early optimism gave way to a period of funding reductions (referred to as "AI winters") as systems failed to meet performance expectations. Rule-based systems found it difficult to handle complex situations. Symbolic logic systems were brittle in realistic environments, and intelligence was much harder to encode than theoretical developers expected. Even though the pursuit of creating AI never ceased, it remained challenging to develop systems that met expectations for several decades.

Statistical learning methods began to outperform symbolic systems in the 1990s, and a dramatic decrease in image recognition errors occurred in 2012 with a deep neural network, indicating that machine learning had reached a new level of applicability. What changed was not just improved accuracy. Scale also changed — large amounts of data were available, computational power was widely available, and algorithms could now learn from millions, then billions of examples.

Artificial intelligence did not rapidly expand into society. It gradually moved into existing infrastructures. Search engines began using statistical patterns to rank search results. E-commerce sites used incremental improvements to recommendation systems to increase conversions by 10-20%. Banks embedded statistical models in the credit risk evaluation process. Hospitals began experimenting with systems that identified potential complications before patients exhibited symptoms. No one held a press conference to announce that intelligence was moving from being uniquely human to a shared resource. There was no single event that marked a turning point. Instead, AI is gradually integrated into existing processes, improving them slightly.

By the time the general public began debating artificial intelligence, it had already been improving decision-making processes for many years.

Today, AI systems influence which news articles appear in a user's feed, which loan applications are approved, which resumes are passed along to humans for review, which advertisements a person sees across multiple platforms, and which medical images are selected for additional review. None of these systems loudly proclaims its authority. They function quietly by continuously adjusting probabilities and ranking options. Influence, however, does not require visible authority.

What has made artificial intelligence historically important is not simply that machines can recognize images or create text. It is that predictive systems now participate in making judgments at scale. Decision-making under limited human attention is increasingly influenced by statistical inference derived from massive datasets.

This book is not intended to either praise or dramatize the transition to AI decision-making. It is intended to help us better understand the transition. Artificial intelligence is typically characterized as a technological achievement. Technology alone, however, cannot fully explain why the pursuit of AI persisted for multiple decades of uncertainty, or why AI today attracts strategic interest from governments, corporations, and academia worldwide. AI exists because people continue to want to formalize, extend, and externalize their abilities. From the development of writing to the creation of calculus, we have continually encoded cognitive processes into systems that transcend individual minds. Artificial intelligence is an expression of that desire to formally describe, extend, and externalize ability into the domains of learning and prediction.

However, when machines begin to suggest, categorize, and create at scale, the conversation quickly expands beyond engineering. Intelligence, previously considered inseparable from consciousness and experience, is now being operationalized. People begin to ask not only how systems function, but also what authority systems should have. When a model predicts risk, to what extent should it be given consideration? When an algorithm determines how information is ranked, in what ways does that affect perception? When a generative system writes a report, who is responsible for the conclusions?

These questions are not abstract. They manifest themselves in procurement policy, regulatory hearings, corporate board meetings, classrooms, hiring pipelines, access to credit, public discourse, and institutional trust. Intelligence that people created now plays a role in determining which opportunities and access are available to individuals. It frequently occurs invisibly, embedded within defaults and automatic workflow processes. Therefore, it is often normalized.

We encode our values and priorities in the systems we design. We expose histories in the data we collect and select. We express what is most important by defining the goals we seek to achieve in the systems we create. AI systems amplify patterns. What we amplify is determined by what we reward.

Therefore, understanding artificial intelligence requires not merely technical literacy, but institutional and historical perspectives. Understanding artificial intelligence requires identifying why we were motivated to pursue machine intelligence for so long. Understanding artificial intelligence requires identifying what presumptions guided its design. Understanding artificial intelligence requires analyzing how its incorporation into current practices shapes our own habits of judgment.

You will not find step-by-step coding instructions in these pages. Instead, you will identify how intelligence is conceptualized, operationalized, and normalized. You will study how human ingenuity creates artificial systems, how artificial systems, in turn, modify human behavior, and how accountability develops as predictions become more abundant.

Artificial intelligence did not arise out of necessity. Artificial intelligence emerged from a purposeful investigation, persistent investment, and collective ambition. Today, the primary issue is not whether machines can learn. A far deeper issue is how we will interact with the intelligence we have developed and what that indicates about us.

CHAPTER ONE
THE IDEA THAT REFUSES TO SLEEP

Every meaningful invention begins the same way: with a thought that refuses to sleep

Long before computers could perform calculations, save data, or detect patterns, humans imagined the possibility of something called "intelligence" beyond their individual selves, not for the sake of efficiency or profit, but out of a fundamental curiosity that characterizes the human mind – namely, questioning what is seen, imagining things that do not exist yet, and wondering if the boundaries that limit us are absolute.

Artificial Intelligence (AI) did not emerge spontaneously with modern computing. Nor did it come into being in one piece, complete with algorithms and datasets. It existed before that time, as an idea — a quiet, insistent inquiry that has accompanied humanity throughout the centuries: What does it mean to think? And if we can understand thinking, can we recreate it? This question was relevant long before it could be addressed. Philosophers debated it long before engineers tried to build it. Mathematicians studied the structure of reasoning before machines could mimic it. In this regard, AI represents the next chapter in a long history of human exploration: the attempt to understand ourselves through the creation of representations of our capabilities beyond our own physicality. What sets artificial intelligence

apart from other tools created by humans is not merely the complexity of the tool itself. Rather, it is the scope of the creators' ambitions. Humans have created tools to enhance our muscle strength, our sensory acuity, and our range of motion. However, AI seeks to enhance an aspect of our cognitive functioning that is far more intrinsic: our judgment, our learning, and our decision-making. As such, AI impacts those areas of our cognitive functions that we previously believed were unique to humans.
For this reason, AI seems different. And that is why we have never been able to ignore it.

BUILDING REFLECTIONS, NOT MINDS

One of the most persistent misunderstandings about artificial intelligence is the belief that machines are becoming human-like. In reality, AI systems are not replicas of the human mind. They are reflections, partial, imperfect, and shaped entirely by human design choices.

Machines do not think the way humans think. They do not experience curiosity, intention, or meaning. They do not understand context in the way people do. What they do exceptionally well is recognize patterns, optimize outcomes, and repeat processes at a scale no human could manage. And yet, in those patterns, something familiar appears.

When we teach machines how to learn, we inevitably encode assumptions about what matters, what should be rewarded, and what should be ignored. The systems we build reflect our priorities, our shortcuts, and sometimes our blind spots. In that sense, AI tells us as much about ourselves as it does about technology.

We learn which decisions we value enough to automate. We learn where we trust data more than judgment. We learn how willing we are to trade explanation for efficiency. Each system becomes a quiet record of human choice. This is not accidental. Artificial intelligence is shaped less by what machines are capable of and more by what humans ask them to do.

THE COMFORT OF DELEGATION

There is yet another reason artificial intelligence continues to be discussed: its promise of relief. Thinking is very tiring; decision-making is physically draining; judging is stressful and risky because you're accountable for your judgments. The notion of Artificial Intelligence is attractive because it allows some of the stress associated with those activities to be transferred to a system. As long as a system can assist you with making decisions, predicting results, etc., the feeling is that the human's workload has been reduced. That was not done immediately, however. It occurred incrementally, and almost as if it were being done out of courtesy. Machines first helped with mathematical computations, then with organizing information, then with providing suggestions for action, and eventually began to influence outcomes. At each point in time, the shift seemed a "reasonable" thing to do. Even helpful, many would say. However, when viewed collectively, the gradual transfer of responsibility to machines fundamentally altered the relationship between man and his tools. Intelligence no longer resided in the individual who used the tool, but began to reside in the tool itself. This alteration in the relationship between man and his tools raises an important, unspoken question: Where does true responsibility lie when a machine assists us in making a decision? This is an unpleasant truth, which is one reason it is frequently ignored. True responsibility does not go away when it is distributed among individuals; it merely becomes more difficult to determine.

The fact that AI continues to surface in our conversations is directly related to how it handles intimate and private matters. AI forces us to ask questions we have never adequately addressed regarding ourselves. We wish to gain insight into intelligence to understand our own minds better. We desire a sense of control, as uncertainty creates discomfort. And we seek to find meaning, as tools that operate only to perform tasks, without values or context, seem to fall short in some manner. AI provides all three of these desires within the same framework, and therefore, there is little chance of avoiding it. It is not that the machine can process information faster than we can; that is unsettling to us. Rather, it is that they cause us to become aware of how much of our own thinking can be translated into formulas and how much of our thinking cannot. They make us uncomfortable with how easily we substitute judgment for expediency and how readily we entrust systems we do not fully understand.

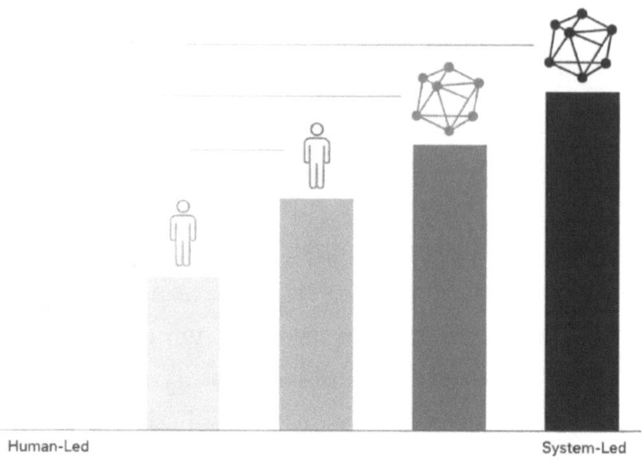

AI raises another quieter concern. When intelligence is removed from human experience, is it neutral, or does it merely represent the values we provided it without questioning? These are not concerns that can be resolved with improved hardware or cleaner software. They continue to exist because they are human issues. They exist in the areas where responsibility, purpose, and accountability converge. This is why discussions surrounding AI tend to evolve into discussions regarding ethics, philosophy, and identity. We are not only discussing what machines can accomplish. We are working through what it means to develop something that can participate in decision-making processes previously performed by humans.

Ultimately, our preoccupation with artificial intelligence is more about self-reflection and less about technology. By developing artificial intelligence, we are compelled to examine ourselves more closely.

THE BEGINNING OF RESPONSIBILITY

The dream of creating intelligent machines will haunt humanity and cannot be put to rest. The true weight of developing AI lies in the responsibilities it entails. Every system is developed based on decisions made by an individual. Every outcome can be traced back to the data selected, the objectives defined, and the priorities established. Artificial intelligence does not develop itself in a vacuum; it is intentionally designed, even if we do not acknowledge this intentionality. Therefore, as you seek to understand artificial intelligence, you need to understand not only how systems function but also why they were developed, what we hope to achieve through them, and what we may be willing to ignore to reap their benefits.

This book is not initiated with code or algorithms. This book began with humans because the intelligence we have created has not emerged solely from the machine. Rather, it has been a result of our own human curiosity, creativity, and desire to improve. As such, artificial intelligence reflects us in ways that we could never anticipate.

.

CHAPTER TWO
THE INTELLIGENCE WE CAN TOUCH

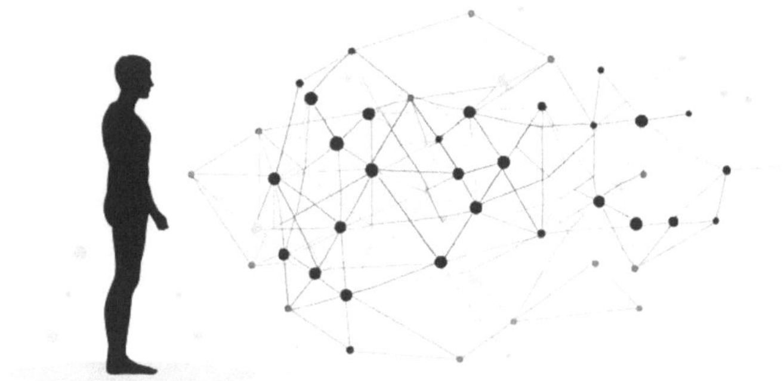

Artificial intelligence became influential not when it grew more powerful, but when it became ordinary.

Most of us think of Artificial Intelligence (AI) as a complicated technological entity found in remote labs or futuristic computer devices. But, in reality, the most impactful AI systems are often those that go unseen and unheard. These AI systems are present in many of the common tools and applications we use daily, helping guide our choices, anticipate outcomes, and direct our actions without ever getting our attention.

This isn't just a coincidence. One of the design tenets guiding the development of contemporary AI systems is minimal intrusiveness, which allows them to blend into daily activities and experiences. This reduces the perception that

intelligence is technology and instead gives the impression that intelligence is a continuation of how humans typically engage with the environment. That is the point at which it begins to really matter. The significance of this shift lies not in the existence of intelligence itself but in the alteration of the conditions under which we make decisions. AI rarely eliminates human choice. Rather, it fundamentally alters the environment within which we make decisions. AI determines which choices are visible to us, which paths are easy to follow, and which outcomes are probable. Artificial intelligence systems determine this through machine learning. Machine learning systems observe patterns in data and learn which options tend to be preferred, which stimuli tend to elicit responses, and which behaviors tend to recur. Over time, machine learning systems develop the ability to anticipate what will happen next; they don't require explicit instruction to operate.
At the point at which AI achieves this level of functionality, it no longer needs to notify anyone that it exists. It doesn't need to command our attention. It simply functions. Because of this reason alone, ordinary AI is far more influential than spectacular AI. While a system that surprises us may impress us once, one that quietly develops a sense of familiarity by adapting to us can easily become habitual.

Our conduct is sustained over extended periods by habits rather than by singular incidents. AI has evolved from being seen as a tool to functioning as infrastructure as a result of its constant integration into the vast array of goods and services we use daily.

Search engines, recommendation systems, predictive text, automated filtering, and personalized feeds all rely on artificial intelligence. However, few users perceive these as examples of AI. Rather, they perceive these as convenience features. While this normalization has both positive and negative implications, there are two primary effects. Firstly, when intelligence becomes ordinary, people cease to ask "how" it works and assume it simply does. Trust is not generated through an individual's understanding of a system. Rather, trust is built on consistency. If a system consistently delivers acceptable results, its internal logic becomes less relevant to the user.

Secondly, this consistent reliability gradually transfers responsibility away from the individual. Choices that previously were deliberated become automatic. Judgments that formerly required focused attention become default settings. While AI does not eliminate human agency, it alters how it is exercised. Instead of making every decision directly, humans increasingly approve, modify, or reject decisions that intelligent systems have already influenced. The role of the human being in this process evolves from generator to supervisor.

This represents a significant transformation in the relationship between humans and intelligence. For much of human history, intelligence was a characteristic that individuals had and applied. Today, however, intelligence is also a source that we interact with, an external force that contributes to our cognitive processing.
It filters the information that we view. It ranks the information we review by relevance before deciding whether

to pursue it further. It predicts the outcome of our actions before we act. Additionally, because this type of intelligence appears to be ordinary, its influence often goes unnoticed.

Therefore, understanding artificial intelligence requires more than merely knowing about algorithms and models. Understanding how intelligence behaves when it becomes ordinary is required. Understanding how it shapes decisions without providing explicit guidance. Understanding how it impacts outcomes without asserting authority.

The impact of the intelligence we build is greatest not when it astonishes us but when it recedes into the background and quietly becomes a component of how we move about the world. At this point, artificial intelligence ceases to be an innovation and becomes a fundamental aspect of modern life.

THE DESIGN CHOICE TO DISAPPEAR

The most influential artificial intelligence systems have never been designed to make a show of their abilities. Instead, they were created to be unremarkable. In many ways, this is ironic, given that breakthrough announcements and public demonstrations of the latest developments so often define the field of artificial intelligence. Still, the AI systems that most fundamentally shape our lives each day are almost always introduced with relatively little fanfare. They come quietly and typically enter through interfaces we already know well, as improvements rather than innovations. This lack of a flashy introduction is neither a design mistake nor a failure of imagination. Rather, it is a deliberate decision.

Early artificial intelligence systems made their intelligence obvious to users. For example, expert systems provided explanations of the reasoning behind their conclusions. Likewise, rule-based systems provided displays of the logical structures supporting their conclusions. Using early AI systems required users to pay attention and exert effort. In other words, users were aware that they were interacting with something that was not human, and that awareness influenced how users treated the system.

In contrast to earlier AI systems, modern AI takes a very different philosophy. Instead of requiring users to adapt to intelligence, modern AI adapts to its users. As such, the interfaces of modern AI are designed to be intuitive. Responses from modern AI are optimized for speed. Decisions generated by modern AI are presented to users in formats that mimic human judgment. The primary goal of this design philosophy is not to demonstrate intelligence, but to eliminate friction. As long as AI can function in the background (i.e., "disappear"), it has succeeded. Both technical realities and human realities motivated this shift. Machine learning models perform optimally when they operate continuously and learn from massive amounts of interaction data. The more users interact with a system naturally, the more interaction data the system collects, and thus the better it is at modeling user behavior. The visibility of AI models during their operation disrupts this loop. The moment users begin paying attention and thus hesitate, friction is introduced, and the rate of feedback decreases.

Therefore, designing AI to "disappear" is not merely about creating comfortable user experiences. It is about maximizing the system's effectiveness. Recommendation engines, ranking algorithms, and predictive systems all depend on the continuous flow of interaction data to produce their best results. These systems are most effective when users do not consciously recognize their presence. Each click, pause, correction, or acceptance made by a user generates additional training data. Thus, the more users use a system naturally, the more data it collects, and consequently, the more accurately it models user behavior. While human-centered design research reinforced this approach to AI design, studies consistently demonstrated that users prefer systems that provide suggestions based upon anticipated needs, without first requiring clarification from the user.

Users are more likely to trust suggestions that appear to be timely and relevant than those that require justification. The smoother the user experience, the more reliable the system appears to the user.

Over time, this design logic has transformed the way users perceive artificial intelligence in their everyday experiences. Artificial intelligence no longer appears as a distinct feature within the tools users employ. Instead, artificial intelligence increasingly appears to users as a normal extension of the tools themselves. As a result, the distinction between software behavior and intelligent behavior has diminished. The implications of this disappearance are profound. When artificial intelligence is hidden, it is significantly more difficult for users to question the system's logic or reasoning. When systems operate seamlessly, users are less likely to ask "why" a particular recommendation was made, "why" an option was ranked higher, or "why" a specific prediction was produced. Therefore, the design strategy that creates the most usable experience also creates the least scrutinized experience.

It does not follow that this design is inherently unethical. Rather, it is extremely powerful. Invisible systems exert considerable influence over user behavior without confrontation. They direct user attention without commanding it. They affect the ultimate outcomes of user-system interactions while preserving the illusion of user agency. Although users continue to choose among options, the environment in which the choices are made has already been shaped by the invisible system. In this context, the disappearance of artificial intelligence is not about hiding the truth, but about alignment. Systems are designed to align with the patterns of human behavior, mental shortcuts, and time constraints. They fit into everyday life without disrupting it.

However, alignment also entails responsibilities. When intelligence is embedded in the interface (rather than being a visible agent), accountability is diffused. The user benefits from convenience. The system experiences optimization. Between the two lies a void where influence occurs silently. Recognizing the design choices underlying artificial intelligence today is essential to understanding the nature of the influence it now exerts worldwide. Artificial intelligence did not gain influence by drawing attention to itself. Rather, it gained influence by disappearing from view and integrating intelligence into mundane actions. The intelligence that humans developed did not decline in influence due to weakness. Rather, it declined in influence because that was the most effective way for it to function.

Once artificial intelligence disappears, however, it continues to exert influence over the world; it simply does so without being perceived.

LEARNING FROM US BEFORE WE NOTICE

Modern artificial intelligence doesn't begin with an understanding of behavior; rather, it starts with observing it. Machine Learning Systems (MLS) are designed to identify patterns in behavior, which occur well before any attempt to understand them. MLS learn from observing what people do, not from questioning why they do it. Each person's interactions create a new data point; each repeated interaction strengthens the pattern.
It is from this ability to strengthen patterns that MLS develops the capacity to predict continually. Unlike traditional software, which uses an explicit set of instructions, MLS learn to predict by adjusting as it is exposed to additional examples of behavior over time. In turn, the system develops the ability to make predictions based on what consistently occurs over time.

The system does not require permission or direction to continue updating; in fact, the process typically occurs quietly and may not even produce an observable indication that learning occurred. In doing so, an inherent asymmetry exists. Individuals are more likely to notice intelligent behavior when it produces unexpected results. However, AI becomes effective when it no longer provides unexpected results and instead produces predictions that appear obvious, expected, or natural. Once the predictions feel as though they have been generated from prior experience and therefore fit naturally within a given routine, the system has reached a level of effectiveness that can be absorbed into the normal flow of activity.

To illustrate this concept, consider the large-scale recommendation systems utilized by online streaming services. These systems initially utilize broad signals such as genre, popularity, and user input. Over time, these systems learn much more detailed behavioral patterns. For example, they will monitor when a user stops viewing, which scenes are viewed multiple times, when content is viewed, and how long the user continues to pay attention to the content. Based on these signals, the system will generate predictions regarding not only what type of content a user may like, but also when the user is most likely to accept the recommended content. Eventually, the recommendations will cease to be perceived as suggestions and instead will appear as inevitable. Typically, users do not search for content; they select from a predetermined list of recommendations. The system has learned enough to predict preferences before the individual consciously recognizes them.

Most users cannot articulate the reasons behind a particular recommendation; they recognize that it "feels right." At this point in the system's development, AI may recognize patterns of behavior before the individual consciously identifies them.

It can identify habits developing, preferences changing, and tendencies that continue to repeat over time. The system's intelligence operates ahead of the individual's awareness. This is not due to AI possessing an understanding of intent or meaning; it does not. It possesses a knowledge of probability. It can determine what is likely to occur next based on past occurrences.

However, when probability is applied at a large scale, it becomes influential. As the system's predictions improve, it begins to frame the sequence of options available to users. Some options are displayed before others, some more frequently than others, and some are visually emphasized while others fade into obscurity. The system does not directly dictate users' actions, but it defines the context in which users' behaviors occur. By the time the user becomes cognizant of the system's influence, the system has already developed the knowledge to shape users' behavior. AI does not require deep knowledge of the individual to influence their behavior; it merely requires consistent knowledge. Consistency is learned long before it is identified.

CHAPTER THREE
WHAT AI LEARN ABOUT US

Artificial Intelligence (AI) has become an integral part of modern business. AI enables companies to automate routine tasks, improve operational efficiency, and make better decisions. But with the emergence of artificial intelligence, we are beginning to see that its applications extend far beyond the confines of business; they are found in many forms of entertainment, medicine, and scientific research. The ability of AI to learn and adjust to novel circumstances while continuously enhancing its performance over time accounts for the wide range of applications it can be used for.

Similarly, as humans learn through experience and experimentation to acquire new knowledge, AI learns by processing large amounts of data. The similarity to the human learning process is most apparent in two concepts that apply to the development of AI skills: neural networks that replicate the function of the human brain and machine learning. Now, let's take a look at how AI learning actually takes place.

Modern AI systems do not create human behavior. They reflect human behavior, magnify it, and scale it. What makes modern AI systems the way they are depends much less on machines than on the patterns people create. In this chapter, we will discuss, from a practical standpoint, what modern AI systems quietly learn about us. Not from theory, but from actual practice.

PATTERNS ARE NOT NEUTRAL

Machine learning systems are trained on historical data. Myriad human choices, tastes, customs, and contradictions shape those data points. Machine Learning has no way of differentiating between intent and result. All observable actions are signals to an AI.

Hiring algorithms, for instance, are trained on a history of hiring and are therefore predisposed to select individuals with qualities similar to those of the people they have hired in the past. Not based on understanding what is good about someone, but rather based on what is successful (repeated). In machine learning, this is called "patterned inheritance". Patterns become rules.

When we say that machines are intelligent, we really mean that the machines can recognize patterns. A very important distinction to make when we consider that these patterns may reflect inequalities, biases, or exclusions. Machines will not remedy the problem. Rather, machines will speed up the process. Machines do not assess whether the actions taken in creating the data should continue. Machines take the data given to them and make it actionable.

Optimization Reveals Value

Every AI system is optimized for something. Accuracy. Engagement. Speed. Retention. Cost reduction. These goals are not neutral technical decisions. They are expressions of human priorities translated into mathematical terms.

Consider social media recommendation systems. They are often optimized for engagement, measured by time spent or interaction frequency. Over time, the system learns which content holds attention most effectively. Not which content is accurate, meaningful, or beneficial, but which content keeps users engaged. This optimization reveals a quiet truth: AI systems reflect the values embedded in their objectives. When engagement becomes the dominant metric, emotional intensity often outperforms nuance. The system is not manipulating users. It is doing exactly what it was designed to do. AI does not hide values. It encodes them.

FEEDBACK LOOPS AND BEHAVIORAL REINFORCEMENT

Once AI systems begin influencing behavior, the data they collect changes. The system no longer learns from neutral observation alone. It learns from the environment it helped shape. This creates feedback loops. A recommendation system promotes certain content. That content receives more attention. The increased attention reinforces the system's belief that the content is valuable. Alternative content receives less exposure and eventually disappears from the dataset. Over time, the system's predictions become self-confirming.

Example: News Ranking Algorithms

If an algorithm prioritizes articles that generate rapid clicks, it will increasingly surface headlines designed for immediacy rather than depth. Readers then engage with what is available, reinforcing the system's model of preference. The intelligence is not wrong. It is consistent. But consistency is not the same as truth.

WHAT THE SYSTEMS KNOW AND WHAT THEY UNDERSTAND

AI systems are exceptionally good at recognizing correlations. They are not good at understanding causes. This gap is often misunderstood.

The system may know:

- When users are likely to disengage
- Which options are usually accepted?
- how behavior shifts across time and context

But it does not know why. This distinction is critical. AI can predict outcomes without understanding meaning. That predictive strength makes it powerful, but also limited.

Below is a simple comparison that clarifies this boundary:

What AI learns	**What AI does not understand**
Behavioral Pattern	Human Intention
Probabilities	Moral Judgement

Correlations	Causations
Optimization outcomes	Contextual significance
Repetition	Purpose

This gap is not a flaw. It is a boundary. Problems arise when predictive confidence is mistaken for comprehension. Artificial intelligence mirrors us at scale. It reveals what we do repeatedly, what we reward unconsciously, and what we prioritize when convenience is available. Understanding AI, therefore, requires understanding ourselves, not as individuals, but as patterns.

The intelligence we built does not ask who we want to be. It shows us who we have been. And what we choose to do with that reflection is where responsibility begins.

CHAPTER FOUR
ETHICS IN THE AGE OF THINKING MACHINES

Artificial Intelligence Does Not Have a Moral Awareness, Therefore It Does Not Hesitate, Reflect, or Question the Consequences of Its Output. Yet it has become involved in many of the same decision-making processes as human beings, including job opportunities, financial options, health care guidance, what we see on social media, and even public safety.

The Ethical Dilemma with artificial intelligence is not how well an artificial intelligence system can think, but rather the degree to which humans put thought into creating systems that are beginning to impact how most people live their lives today. In today's world, ethics is not decorative philosophy, but rather architectural engineering.

THE LIMITS OF ETHICS BY DESIGN

In the development of artificial intelligence, a reassuring belief has become common: if ethical principles are embedded into systems during design, the resulting technology will behave responsibly. Fairness constraints can be added. Transparency mechanisms can be implemented. Bias can be audited. Accountability can be documented.

The idea is simple and attractive: to solve ethics at the engineering level. This approach, often described as "ethics by design," assumes that moral challenges can be translated into technical specifications. If we refine the model carefully enough, the ethical risk will be minimized.

But this belief rests on a narrow understanding of how AI systems operate in the world.

Artificial intelligence does not exist as isolated code. It functions inside institutions, markets, regulatory gaps, and cultural assumptions. A technically improved system may still produce harmful outcomes when deployed within flawed structures. Ethics cannot end at the moment of design.

When Complex Values Become Technical Variables

Designing ethical AI requires translating human values into measurable criteria. Fairness becomes a statistical metric. Accountability becomes a documentation requirement. Transparency becomes an explainability feature.

These translations are necessary. Machines cannot process ambiguity. They require formal definitions. The difficulty arises when rich moral concepts are reduced to quantifiable thresholds. Take fairness as an example. In technical systems, fairness may be defined as equal error rates across demographic groups or balanced representation within datasets. These definitions are important and often improve measurable outcomes.

Yet fairness in society is broader than statistical parity. It includes historical disadvantage, structural inequality, context, and lived experience. A system can satisfy a fairness constraint mathematically while still operating within an environment shaped by deep inequality. When values are reduced to variables, ethical compliance can replace ethical reflection.

The system may be optimized correctly according to its defined metric, but the metric itself may be incomplete. Ethics by design often assumes that once values are formalized and encoded, the problem is contained. In reality, encoding values is only the beginning of a much larger conversation.

The Illusion of Control in Complex Systems

Another limitation of ethics by design exists in the inherent assumption of predictability. Ethics by design assumes that, as long as the designer provides input and adjusts the appropriate parameters, the system's outcome will develop predictably.

However, AI operates within a dynamic environment. Users interact with recommendation systems, which in turn cause them to adapt. Organizations interact with automated systems, which then adjust their policies accordingly. Prediction systems impact markets. Feedback loops develop over time. Small design decisions made during the development of a system can have large unintended consequences once the system is scaled. For example, an applicant tracking system (ATS) designed to eliminate bias in the candidate selection process may create new biases in how applicants create resumes for ATS systems. Similarly, an ATS may introduce a new bias in how recruiters evaluate candidates through the applicant's resume profile. In addition, a hiring decision based on a merit-based system may result in a different definition of merit than existed before the implementation of the ATS.

While a content moderation system may remove the identified harmful content from online platforms, it may also create a new normative standard for communication. As such, the designer of the content moderation system typically does not have complete control over all downstream impacts. Ethics by design focuses on improving the artifact, i.e., the system itself.

AI is not simply an artifact. It is an intervention into a living social system. Complex systems do not behave in a strictly predictable manner. Rather, they respond to, adapt to, and evolve as a result of interaction, not simply as a result of the intentions of those who develop them. Therefore, the ethical responsibility for developing complex systems should not be limited to the initial design decisions. Rather, ethical responsibility should continue throughout the system's life cycle and include ongoing monitoring, institutional accountability, and a willingness to revise or withdraw the system when unintended harm emerges. Embedding ethics into code is important.

However, believing that code alone can represent ethical responsibility is not. The limitations of ethics by design serve as a reminder that AI is both a technological innovation and a social force. As such, the oversight required to ensure that AI is developed and deployed responsibly must extend well beyond the engineering phase.

PARTICIPATION WITHOUT POWER

The language of inclusiveness has been adopted by numerous organizations in response to the growing concerns around artificial intelligence. We now hear calls for participatory design, diverse datasets, community consultation, and inclusive innovation. On the surface, these developments signal progress. They suggest that AI systems will be shaped not only by engineers and executives, but also by the communities affected by them. Participation is the ethical solution to the concentration of technological power. Yet participation does not automatically produce influence.

In many cases, communities are invited to provide feedback, share data, or contribute lived experience without being granted meaningful authority over final decisions. Workshops are held. Surveys are distributed. Public consultations are announced. But the core objectives, deployment timelines, and economic incentives often remain unchanged. Input is collected. Direction is preserved. This dynamic creates a subtle imbalance. Participation becomes symbolic rather than structural. It legitimizes systems without redistributing control.

Consultation Versus Decision-Making Power

There is an important distinction between being heard and having power. Being heard means offering perspective. Having power means shaping outcomes.

In AI development, the most consequential decisions involve:

- What problems are prioritized
- What objectives are optimized
- Where systems are deployed
- Who bears risk?
- Who benefits economically?

These decisions are typically made at organizational and executive levels, far removed from those invited to "participate."

Consider predictive technologies introduced into public institutions, such as schools, police systems, or welfare distribution systems. Communities may be consulted about concerns or implementation preferences. But rarely are they given authority to reject deployment altogether. Participation without veto power is limited. The ethical question, therefore, is not whether consultation occurs. It is whether affected communities possess meaningful agency within technological decision-making processes. Without structural influence, participation risks becoming a tool for legitimacy rather than justice.

The Global Imbalance of AI Development

Globalization and the Power Imbalance of Advanced AI
The extent to which the distribution of power can be seen to become even more apparent at the global level is by how advanced AI technologies are primarily developed in technologically superior countries that have the necessary financial backing for large-scale computing, as well as both physical and virtual data storage systems; these technologies are then distributed throughout the globe in many cases in environments where there are very different cultural values, laws and policies regarding personal freedoms and social priorities. In such environments, communities will use and interact with AI systems that were designed with little or no input from them and, in many cases, developed with support from laws and regulations that do not exist in their environment.
AI Language Models That Are Predominantly Trained Using Data from Specific Regions May Incorporate Cultural Assumptions

For example, facial recognition technology developed in jurisdictions that provide a high degree of protection for citizens' rights may be used in other jurisdictions with weaker protections. Personal information provided to companies operating AI systems worldwide may be stored, processed, and sold in jurisdictions with less stringent protections for individuals' rights, even those who may never have had the opportunity to consent to the collection and sale of their data.

In addition to creating an imbalance of power among individuals and corporations, this also creates an imbalance of power among regions of the world. Participation Is Important

Participation can help create diversity of thought and experiences in the development process. Diversity of thought and experience can lead to increased awareness of potential problems that may arise when using an AI system. However, broader representation can identify issues that would otherwise go unaddressed in the development process. However, while it is important to listen to diverse perspectives, it is equally important to shift the balance of power. Unless there is a structural change in the way decision-making authority is distributed, participation can remain procedural rather than truly representative. The artificial intelligence (AI) systems we develop today reflect not only our technical sophistication but also our existing power structures. Unless the participation in the development of AI systems changes the power structure, the development of AI systems will be ethically incomplete.

A MULTI-LEVEL FRAMEWORK FOR RESPONSIBILITY

If ethics in artificial intelligence is confined to model design, it remains incomplete. If participation does not shift power, it remains symbolic. If infrastructure is ignored, the impact is underestimated. What becomes clear is this: responsibility in the age of thinking machines operates across multiple levels simultaneously.

Artificial intelligence is not a single object. It is a layered system. And each layer carries its own ethical demands. To govern AI responsibly, we must understand these layers.

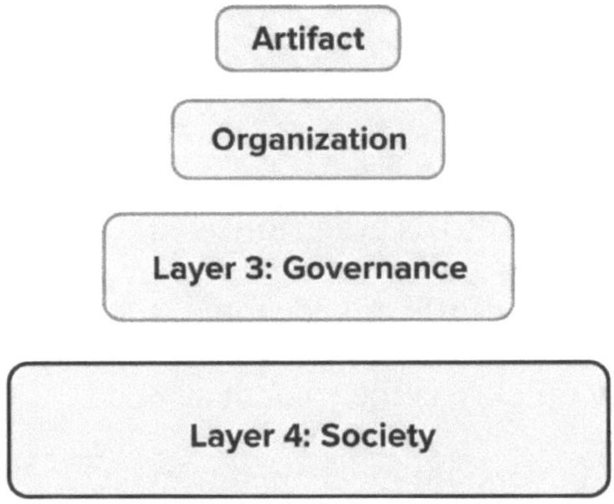

The Artifact Level: The System Itself

At the most visible level lies the AI system as artifact: the model, the dataset, the algorithm.

This is where most technical ethical interventions occur:

- Bias testing
- Fairness metrics
- Explainability tools
- Safety constraints
- Performance auditing

These efforts are necessary. They address how the system behaves under defined conditions. They seek to minimize harm within measurable boundaries. But this level answers only one question: *Is the system functioning as intended?*

It does not address whether the intention itself is appropriate.

The Organizational Level: Incentives and Deployment

Above the artifact lies the organization that builds and deploys the system.

Here, ethical questions shift toward:

- What objectives are prioritized?
- What trade-offs are accepted?
- How quickly is the system scaled?
- What oversight mechanisms exist?
- Who is accountable when harm occurs?

An ethically designed model can still produce harm if deployed under pressure to maximize growth, reduce costs, or dominate markets. Organizational incentives shape system behavior as much as technical architecture does. If profit, efficiency, or engagement are rewarded above all else, AI systems will reflect those priorities.

Responsibility at this level requires governance structures, internal accountability, and leadership willing to align strategy with long-term societal impact.

The Societal Level: Law, Culture, and Power

Beyond organizations lies the broader societal environment in which AI operates.

This includes:

- Regulatory frameworks
- Legal protections
- Cultural norms

- Public awareness
- Economic structures

AI systems influence employment patterns, public discourse, institutional decision-making, and civic trust. These effects are not isolated incidents; they reshape social systems over time.

Ethical governance at the societal level requires more than corporate policy. It requires public institutions capable of oversight, democratic debate about acceptable use, and mechanisms to protect vulnerable populations. Without societal guardrails, technological capability can outpace collective consent.

The Ontological Level: What We Believe About Intelligence

The deepest layer is rarely discussed. It concerns how AI reshapes our understanding of intelligence itself.

When we build systems that predict, classify, generate, and decide, we implicitly redefine what thinking means. We risk equating intelligence solely with pattern recognition. We may treat human judgment as inefficient compared to machine optimization.

These assumptions influence education, employment, and self-perception. If intelligence becomes synonymous with data processing speed and predictive accuracy, qualities such as empathy, moral reasoning, and contextual understanding may be undervalued. Ethics at this level asks not only how AI behaves, but how it changes our conception of ourselves.

The intelligence we build shapes the intelligence we admire.

Responsibility Across Layers

Each level, artifact, organization, society, and worldview interact with the others. A flaw at one layer cannot always be corrected at another. A technically fair system cannot compensate for exploitative incentives. Strong regulation cannot compensate for cultural complacency. Inclusive design cannot correct flawed assumptions about intelligence. Ethical AI requires coherence across levels.

Responsibility is not a single action. It is an ongoing alignment between technical design, institutional governance, public oversight, and human values. Artificial intelligence magnifies human intention. It scales what we reward. It accelerates what we prioritize. If responsibility is fragmented, harm is amplified. If responsibility is layered and deliberate, AI can serve rather than destabilize. The age of thinking machines demands more than smarter systems. It demands a clearer understanding of who we are at every level of the systems we build.

CHAPTER FIVE
WHEN DECISIONS STOP BEING HUMAN

There is a point in history when decision-making left evidence of a human presence. Managers evaluated resumes, doctors assessed patients' symptoms, judges reviewed the cases, editors decided which articles would be published, etc. Although they were imperfect, their imperfections were identifiable as human. All the decisions made today, whether or not they reflect human consideration, are created by systems based on probabilities, not reflection. These changes have been developed over time.

They have not occurred quickly through the development of convenience and scale. Humans are no longer directly making all the decisions; we are just in different positions.

THE RISE OF PREDICTIVE AUTHORITY

Modern AI systems are designed to forecast. They estimate the likelihood of certain outcomes, such as: Who is most likely to repay a loan? Which applicant will likely succeed? Which kind of content has the most chance of capturing viewers' attention? Which behaviors are most likely to occur? Often in our work, forecasting (predicting) is influential. If a model consistently produces accurate predictions on a large dataset, its recommendations can be considered authoritative. Statistical confidence has replaced individual intuition for many organizations. The way we make decisions has changed as a result.

Rather than inquiring, "What do we think?" We have started inquiring, "What does the model tell us?"

Credit scoring systems provide a good example of this concept. Many decisions about an individual's access to financial resources are made using predictive risk assessments developed from algorithms trained on past repayment data. The system does not understand the aspirational nature of the individual, the impact of sudden hardship, or how the individual utilizes informal economic means to survive; it understands probability.

Although the system appears objective in its decision, it still determines an individual's opportunities. Once predictive systems are used as the primary reference points, the authority to determine the direction of deliberative processes is transferred from humans to statistical outputs. Thus, prediction is becoming the precursor to judgment.

FROM DECISION-MAKER TO SYSTEM SUPERVISOR

As AI systems grow more integrated into institutional processes, the human role often shifts from decision-maker to supervisor.

A recruiter reviews candidates pre-filtered by automated ranking.
A physician examines diagnoses highlighted by machine analysis.
A content moderator evaluates posts that detection systems have already classified.

Although the human is still present in the process, the choices available to the human are already determined by the previous structural changes. There will be consequences for the changes in how the field of possibilities is defined. The way the system defines the field of possibilities, as a result of framing, will affect human judgment: it will become reactive rather than independent. It will confirm, adjust, or override machine-generated possibilities. This dynamic could, over time, lead to a decrease in cognitive diversity in decision-making. As long as the machine continues to guide where to focus your attention, you will begin to lose sight of alternative explanations for the data. The machine also has limited human accountability.

The machine limits the scope of choice (horizon) for the human.

EFFICIENCY AND THE DISAPPEARANCE OF FRICTION

Automated decision-making has increased because technology enables more efficient processes. Automated decision-making allows companies to process data faster than humans. It also eliminates the cost of manual tasks and creates consistency by using the same logic to evaluate multiple applications. Once friction disappeared, so did deliberation. With no wait time, applicants could not explain their reasoning. With no discussion time, applicants could not justify their decisions. Before automated decision-making, manual reviews allowed applicants to reconsider their decision.

Today, as efficiency continues to increase, reflection may be seen as inefficient. That doesn't mean that automated decision-making is inherently bad. Automated decision-making can create fairness where inconsistent behavior by decision-makers previously existed. However, if the primary consideration is speed, then the depth of the decision-making process may decrease. Automated systems will probably make large-scale decisions that affect thousands of people. An error committed by a system would have far more detrimental effects than a single poor choice made by a person.

THE SUBTLE SHIFT IN MORAL OWNERSHIP

Perhaps the most profound change occurs in how responsibility is perceived.

When a human makes a decision, accountability is direct. A person can explain their reasoning, justify their choices, and accept the consequences. When a system produces an output, responsibility becomes distributed. Designers built the model. Engineers tuned it. Executives approved deployment. Operators implemented it. Users generated the data.

Who, then, owns the decision?

Institutions often speak of "the algorithm" as if the "algorithm" were a person (actor) with its own values.

Algorithms do not have values, nor can they be said to have moral agency. What algorithms do is follow instructions based on the values and goals of the humans who created them, as well as the historical data used in their development. The problem is not when decisions become less obviously made by humans; it is when we begin to lose track of whose values those decisions reflect.

There is no evil intent in the implementation of artificial intelligence (AI). There is merely the normalization of detachment from the consequences of one's actions. If people perceive those decisions are made by impartial systems rather than by human-defined priorities, the ethical scrutiny of those decisions decreases. Decisions then are primarily procedural (i.e., done according to rules) rather than reflective.

While AI does not eliminate decision-making, it changes how decision-making occurs. Some decisions continue to be made entirely by humans, while others may be partially or entirely influenced, filtered, or executed by predictive systems operating at large scales. The changes that are occurring are not revolutionary but incremental. We trust models because they are efficient. We use automation because it is scalable. We accept statistical authority because it appears to be objective.

However, every time an automated decision is made, there is always a trail of human design, institutional incentives, and history that precedes it. When decisions appear to be made by machines (algorithms), they still are made by humans. The issue is whether we will recognize this fact.

CHAPTER SIX
CO-CREATING THE FUTURE

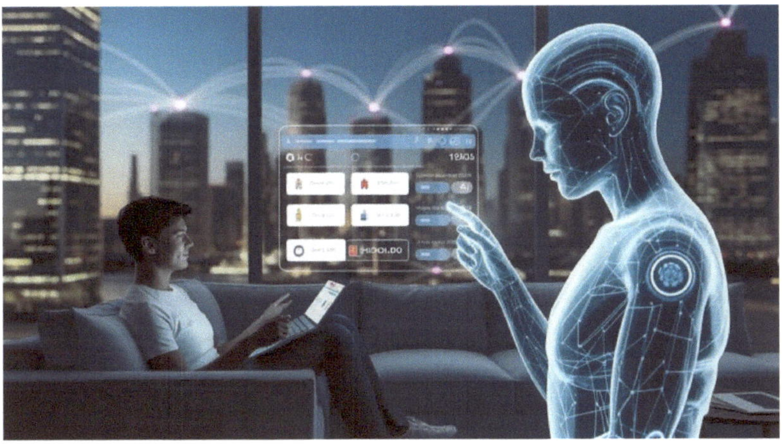

Something subtly changed in 2016 when AlphaGo beat Lee Sedol in a game of Go. The occasion was presented as a victory for neural networks and reinforcement learning, and as a turning point in machine intelligence. However, the fact that the system prevailed was not the only thing many researchers later noticed. It played that way.

Move 37 in Game 2 was described by commentators as unconventional, even irrational, until its long-term brilliance became clear. Human players later studied the move and began incorporating similar strategies into their own games. The machine had not merely defeated a human champion. It had expanded the field's strategic imagination.

That moment offered a glimpse of something important: the future of AI would not be defined solely by replacement. It would also be defined by interaction. Artificial intelligence does not evolve in isolation. It reshapes the humans who engage with it. And in turn, human institutions reshape the systems we build next. Co-creation is not a slogan. It is already happening, whether we acknowledge it or not. The real question is whether we deliberately guide that process.

FROM REACTIVE ADOPTION TO INTENTIONAL DESIGN

For much of the digital era, technology has followed a familiar pattern: build first, regulate later. Social media platforms scaled globally before serious conversations about misinformation, polarization, or mental health consequences emerged. Data collection expanded before meaningful privacy frameworks solidified.

Artificial intelligence initially followed the same trajectory. Startups raced to deploy predictive models in hiring, finance, education, and healthcare. Efficiency gains were immediate. Scale was intoxicating. Investors were enthusiastic. But in boardrooms and engineering meetings, a different conversation began to surface.

I have seen product teams launch AI systems with clear performance benchmarks, accuracy above 92%, latency below 200 milliseconds, and minimized cost per inference. What was rarely quantified was long-term institutional dependency. Once a hospital integrates a diagnostic AI tool deeply into its workflow, removing it becomes difficult. Once a financial institution automates risk assessment, the capacity for human review shrinks. Adoption creates path dependence.

Co-creating the future means shifting from reactive integration to intentional design. It requires asking difficult questions before deployment:

- What human capability are we strengthening?
- What human capability might weaken over time?
- If this system fails, who absorbs the consequences?
- How reversible is this integration?

These are not engineering questions alone. They are governance questions.

The future will not be shaped only by what we can build. It will be shaped by what we choose to institutionalize.

DESIGNING SYSTEMS THAT STRENGTHEN HUMAN JUDGMENT

One of the most interesting debates within AI research today is not about scale; it is about alignment and augmentation. Some technologists argue that the ultimate aim is to build systems that surpass human intelligence across domains. Others, particularly in applied AI sectors such as healthcare and public policy, emphasize collaborative intelligence: systems designed to support, not override, human reasoning. In radiology, for example, studies have shown that AI-assisted diagnosis often performs best when human clinicians and models work together. The AI flags anomalies with high sensitivity. The physician interprets context, patient history, and edge cases. Neither performs optimally in isolation. This is not accidental.

AI systems are excellent at statistical generalization across large datasets. Humans are excellent at contextual interpretation, especially in atypical cases. When unusual circumstances arise, such as rare diseases, atypical financial profiles, and complex social factors, human judgment still carries unique weight. The danger arises when institutions treat AI outputs as the default truth rather than as informed suggestions.

I have spoken with professionals in hiring and financial services who admit privately that once a predictive score is displayed on a dashboard, it exerts gravitational pull. Even if labeled as "decision support," the numerical output influences perception. A candidate with a lower model score is unconsciously viewed through a different lens.

Co-creation requires conscious counterbalance. It means designing systems where:

- Confidence intervals are visible.
- Uncertainty is explicit.
- Human override is meaningful, not symbolic.
- Edge cases are examined deliberately.

When AI systems are framed as collaborators rather than arbiters, human judgment remains active.

THE LITERACY GAP AND THE CONCENTRATION OF INFLUENCE

A recurring challenge in AI governance is asymmetry of understanding.

Inside AI research labs and enterprise engineering teams, conversations are highly specific. Teams debate model drift when real-world data diverges from the training data. They analyze overfitting, in which a system performs impressively on test data but fails under new conditions. They test for adversarial robustness, knowing that minor input manipulations can produce unexpected outputs. They argue over dataset representativeness, threshold tuning, and fairness trade-offs. There is constant awareness that performance metrics are conditional, that models degrade over time, and that no deployment remains static.

Outside those environments, the language shifts dramatically. Artificial intelligence is framed either as a revolutionary force that will solve systemic problems or as an existential threat that will dismantle institutions. The nuance collapses. The probabilistic becomes definitive. The conditional becomes absolute. This gap is not merely rhetorical. It shapes governance. When policymakers do not understand that a model's accuracy is context-dependent, they may regulate based on exaggerated expectations. When they do not grasp that performance degrades as environments change, they may fail to require continuous monitoring. When they misunderstand that optimization requires trade-offs, they may demand systems that are simultaneously maximally accurate, perfectly fair, fully explainable, and infinitely scalable, goals that are often technically in tension with one another.

In practice, AI systems operate within constraints. According to one statistical definition, increasing fairness may reduce predictive accuracy. Improving explainability may limit model complexity. Strengthening privacy protections may reduce the availability of training data. These are not moral failures; they are structural realities of statistical systems. If those realities are not understood at the policy level, regulation can oscillate between overreach and paralysis.

Public misunderstanding produces a different distortion. When AI systems are presented as near-omniscient, trust inflates beyond reasonable limits. People assume predictive models are objective arbiters rather than pattern recognizers trained on historical data. Decisions begin to feel inevitable because they are data-driven. The aura of computation replaces scrutiny.

Conversely, when high-profile failures occur, trust can collapse just as quickly. A biased hiring model or a flawed facial recognition deployment becomes evidence, in the public mind, that all AI systems are fundamentally unreliable. The absence of conceptual literacy prevents calibrated judgment.

What is missing is a middle ground: the recognition that AI systems are powerful but bounded, useful but imperfect, scalable but context-dependent.

Models do not understand meaning; they detect statistical regularities. They do not form intentions; they minimize loss functions. They do not discover truth; they approximate patterns within the limits of their training data. When a language model produces coherent text, it is not reasoning in the human sense. It is predicting token sequences based on learned distributions. When a risk model assigns a probability score, it is not assessing moral character. It estimates the likelihood based on correlations.

Without widespread understanding of these mechanisms, debates become ideological rather than informed.

The literacy gap also concentrates power. When technical knowledge remains confined to a small professional class, oversight becomes dependent on that same class. Regulators rely heavily on industry expertise. Journalists rely on company briefings. Public discourse relies on simplified narratives.

This dynamic is not unique to AI, but the speed and scale of AI deployment magnify its consequences. Unlike earlier industrial technologies, AI systems often operate invisibly within digital infrastructure. Their outputs appear seamless. Their internal logic remains opaque to most users. This invisibility increases reliance on those who design and maintain them.

In countries where digital education includes foundational AI concepts, governance discussions tend to shift from abstract fear toward concrete design questions. Instead of asking whether AI is good or bad, stakeholders ask under what conditions it is appropriate. Instead of framing systems as autonomous actors, they examine the incentives, data sources, and accountability structures that shape them. Where AI is treated as technological mysticism, debate becomes polarized. Systems are either embraced uncritically or rejected wholesale. In both cases, nuance disappears.

Co-creation depends on shared comprehension because governance requires informed participation. If citizens cannot distinguish between predictive modeling and deterministic judgment, they cannot meaningfully challenge automated decisions. If policymakers cannot interpret model limitations, they cannot craft proportionate regulation. If institutions cannot assess uncertainty, they may deploy systems beyond their safe operating boundaries.

The future of AI will not be determined solely by breakthroughs in architecture or scale. It will also be shaped by how widely understanding is distributed.

When knowledge is concentrated, power consolidates. When understanding spreads, direction becomes negotiable. Artificial intelligence may be complex, but its governance cannot remain the exclusive domain of those who build it. Shared literacy is not an accessory to ethical AI. It is a precondition for democratic control over the intelligence we have created.

LONG-TERM INCENTIVES IN A SHORT-TERM MARKET

As far as I can tell, almost all my experiences with AI applications come down to one issue: the push to grow rapidly vs. the need to consider the potential long-term implications of such growth. While most of the pressures to grow rapidly are not necessarily malevolent, they are largely structural. For example, start-ups operate within the venture capital model, which has very short funding-round timelines. Venture capitalists want to see growth in users and usage (engagement) and some level of "proof of concept" and/or "traction." In other words, showing that a model works at small scales is not sufficient; venture capitalists expect to see rapid scaling of the model to many markets. As such, the rewards for expanding, not reflecting, are substantial.

Public companies operate under a similar but equally compressed timeline. Quarterly earnings reports largely determine executive decision-making. Thus, if an AI-driven system increases efficiency by three percent in a single quarter, it will be reflected in the bottom line (margins). However, if that same system causes subtle degradation in institutional judgment over five years, that loss is unlikely to show up in a company's financial statements.

Governments operate under a third but similarly compressed timeline. Governments in particular see AI as strategic infrastructure. Therefore, it may be seen as a sign of weakness to postpone the implementation of an AI application. Thus, a "deployment-first, refine later" mentality may result from the urge to implement AI quickly in order to establish "strategic infrastructure".

These incentives accelerate timelines. These incentives accelerate timelines. While an optimization engine designed to maximize user engagement is not, by itself, going to revolutionize public discourse, it will adjust the ranking weights used by the recommendation engine. It will learn from user click behavior and privilege certain patterns of attention. As a result of these micro-adjustments over time, the optimization engine can influence what content becomes visible, what trends develop, and which fade. Similarly, cultural discourse develops gradually as the result of statistical reinforcement loops. For example, while a predictive policing model may initially seem like a neutral tool for allocating police patrol resources based on historical crime data, the effect of increased police presence in certain areas can be to raise reported crime rates due to increased observation of those areas. Those additional observations create additional data that can feed back into the model to reinforce the initial resource allocation. Through repeated iterations of this process over many years, this recursive process can institutionalize the patterns of resource allocation that appear to be driven by data, but are actually driven by institutionalized practices.

Similarly, a generative model introduced into education as a writing assistant can start by helping students draft ideas, summarize texts, or correct grammar. However, through repeated use, students can develop a habit of relying on the model to perform tasks that would otherwise require them to engage in compositional thinking. This reliance on the model can lead to a gradual shift in the way students approach their own compositional work, i.e., by shifting the cognitive effort required for the task from composition to editing the output generated by the machine.

These types of transformations do not occur suddenly or dramatically. Rather, they occur incrementally and can be difficult to detect. They are not catastrophic failures of AI systems, but rather a gradual transformation in how people interact with technology, including AI systems. The problem is that most short-term metrics (e.g., user engagement, deployment speed, etc.) do not provide adequate insight into how the system will behave in the long run. A system's engagement rate does not indicate whether it is increasing epistemological diversity. A fast adoption curve does not indicate how dependent institutions will become on the system. A high level of cost savings does not indicate whether the use of the system will reduce the need for human expertise in the automated area.

In the engineering phase of developing an AI system, teams tend to focus on model-related issues, such as accuracy, latency, robustness, and scalability. After the AI system is deployed, however, the focus tends to shift from optimizing the model to using metrics that reflect the system's adoption (i.e., how many users are using it) and its performance relative to revenue or efficiency measures. Relatively few organizations spend significant amounts of money on longitudinal studies of how the long-term interactions with

AI systems affect user behavior. As a result of prioritizing short-term metrics over long-term considerations, the unintended consequences of deploying an AI system can compound, as early design decisions are amplified by the feedback loops that develop over time.

Choices made today to optimize an algorithm for "convenience" or "efficiency" can become part of the fabric of institutional practice tomorrow. Optimization objectives set to drive growth this quarter can fundamentally shape the patterns of culture and behavior over the next decade. This is not an argument against innovation. This is an argument for considering the temporal responsibilities associated with introducing technology into society. Extending the evaluation window to consider long-term impacts requires fundamental structural changes. It requires that organizations conduct longitudinal assessments of the impact of their AI applications, not just a one-time review of the ethics of the application.

It requires that organizations revisit their deployed systems periodically to assess how they are drifting, adapting, and creating secondary effects. It requires that organizations have institutional structures in place to stop or reorient a deployed system when the cumulative negative effects of the system become apparent. It also requires that organizations understand that not all technologically possible capabilities should be deployed immediately.

There is often an unstated assumption in the field that if something can be developed and provides a competitive advantage, it will ultimately be developed and deployed.

However, the mere fact that a generative model can produce synthetic persuasive media does not mean that it should be released without restriction. Similarly, the fact that a decision can be automated does not mean that human oversight should be eliminated. In this context, restraint is not anti-progress. Restraint is prudent maturity. There are certainly instances where some forms of optimization may require limits on the optimization. There are certainly cases where some deployments may require staged releases. There are certainly capabilities that will require the establishment of governance frameworks before widespread deployment.

These options may appear to be cautious or conservative in the short term. However, in the long term, they will serve to maintain institutional integrity and public confidence. The intelligence we build advances at accelerating speeds. Society, however, evolves more slowly. If we permit market-based timelines to determine the pace of our intelligence deployment, we risk creating a gap between the speed at which our intelligence accelerates and the pace at which society adapts.

To co-create the future, we must ensure that the speed of innovation is synchronized with the pace of collective reflection. Rapid movement is powerful, but sustained directional movement is determinative.

CHOOSING THE DIRECTION OF INTELLIGENCE

What role does artificial intelligence (AI) represent? This question is debated in academic and policy arenas. The debate is not about the technology behind AI; it is about its philosophy and structure. Does AI represent an efficiency device intended to lower costs and raise productivity? Is AI a competitive advantage in the global fight for technological superiority? Is AI a type of platform technology, such as the Internet, that allows multiple service systems to develop? Or is AI something more fundamental—a new layer of cognitive infrastructure that will quietly affect how society reasons, decides, and organizes? The way you answer that question will determine where AI goes.

In private-sector strategic planning sessions, AI is often viewed as an optimization engine. It improves companies' conversion rates, helps predict customer churn, enhances pricing models, and increases operational efficiency. Within this context, the purpose of AI is clear—maximize measurable returns. Research investments flow toward scalability, performance, and deployment speed. Companies compete based on who can differentiate themselves best. The company's proprietary models become assets. As long as AI is viewed solely as a commercial accelerator, the design priorities of these systems will be driven by market logic. Systems will be optimized to keep customers engaged because engaged customers generate revenue. Models will be trained using data that can be legally and economically obtained. The risk tolerance will align with the company's growth goals. The system's horizon will be determined by the competitive pressures the company faces.

There is nothing inherently wrong with commercial innovation. The majority of AI's rapid advancement has been due to private investment. However, if the commercial orientation becomes predominant, the development of AI will reflect market values more than civic values.

A second perspective on AI began to emerge in the policy arena: AI as civic infrastructure. When electricity was first commercialized, it was also a private enterprise. Eventually, societies realized that energy access was essential to both economic participation and social stability. Regulatory frameworks were created. Public utilities were established. Standards were implemented to ensure the safety, reliability, and equitable access to electricity. A similar pattern may occur if AI becomes integrated into healthcare triage systems, public education platforms, transportation logistics, environmental monitoring, and administrative governance. At that point, AI would begin to look like infrastructure rather than a product. At that point, the criteria for evaluating AI would shift from engagement metrics to reliability, transparency, and accountability.

Some governments are currently developing public-sector AI initiatives focused on medical imaging support in national health systems, climate modeling for environmental resilience, and language tools for multilingual public services. These public sector AI initiatives prioritize accessibility and long-term societal benefit rather than advertising revenue or customer profiling. Under this framework, AI is no longer merely a tool for gaining a competitive advantage. Instead, AI becomes a structural component of society's scaffolding.

Conversation is now beginning to occur regarding AI. The framework for viewing AI is important because it impacts investment priorities, regulatory responses, and public expectations. If AI is viewed primarily as private property, governance may focus on issues related to liability and competition law. If AI is viewed as infrastructure, then governance will expand to include issues such as equity, interoperability standards, auditability, and long-term sustainability.

There is a deeper level of framework that some researchers suggest exists: AI as cognitive infrastructure. Unlike other industrial technologies that amplified physical labor, AI amplifies specific types of reasoning. AI filters information, ranks its relevance, generates text, predicts behavior, and assists decision-making. By doing so, AI mediates how institutions process knowledge. If AI systems continue to influence what information is available to users, which candidates are selected for consideration, which patients receive priority treatment, or which risks are identified, then AI is not simply a tool—it is an intermediary of judgment.

Cognitive infrastructure that shapes decision-making carries a different ethical burden than infrastructure that provides electricity. Cognitive infrastructure affects how societies deliberate and how individuals understand their world. The direction of AI is not predetermined. Rather, the direction of AI results from incentives.

We build intelligence that reflects what we value. If organizations value engagement above all else, systems will evolve to capture user attention efficiently. If organizations value predictive accuracy alone, models will evolve to improve their correlation regardless of the nuances of each context. If regulatory frameworks and institutional cultures value long-term societal stability, then systems can be designed with resilience and equity in mind.

In research laboratories, I have witnessed research teams pivot dramatically in response to the funding structures that exist to incentivize them. When funding structures incentivize speed and scale, architectures evolve to support those characteristics. When funding structures prioritize fairness and interpretability, research agendas shift toward creating explainable models and mitigating biases. Funding structures shape innovation pathways.

Co-creating begins with articulating values because values define the metrics that guide evaluation, and the metrics define what is optimized. Societies must articulate what they want AI to prioritize to avoid allowing the default to be set by those with the greatest concentration of resources. Artificial intelligence does not have an inherent direction; it acquires direction from the environment in which it is funded, deployed, and normalized. Ultimately, whether AI becomes primarily an instrument of commercial acceleration, a regulated public utility, or a carefully managed layer of cognitive infrastructure will depend less on the next technological breakthrough and more on the choices made collectively by society.

The future of AI will reflect not only what is technically feasible, but what is institutionally encouraged and socially protected.

CHAPTER SEVEN
THE LEGACY OF OUR INTELLIGENCE

Every new transformative technology ultimately moves from the lab to institutions. Once that happens, the true impact of that new technology becomes apparent.

Artificial Intelligence (AI) has now reached that point. The results of benchmark competitions, academic advancements, or speculative media headlines are no longer defining AI. Instead, AI is defined by the extent to which it has been incorporated into financial systems, healthcare infrastructures, judicial processes, defense strategies, educational pipelines, and corporate governance frameworks.

The long-term impact of artificial intelligence will not depend on what it can technically accomplish in isolation. The long-term impact of artificial intelligence will result from how it affects decision-making across all institutions that shape the human experience. That process has already begun.

PERFORMANCE METRICS TO STRUCTURAL INFLUENCE

In the early 2010s, after Deep Learning Systems began performing better than traditional Statistical Models in Image Recognition and Language Processing, Performance Gains were described primarily in terms of Accuracy.

Achieving an accuracy rate of 15% versus 26% on Large Datasets represented Scientific Progress. The scientific progress made was Real, and deservedly celebrated. Accuracy was Never the End Goal. Accuracy was always a Gateway to Deployment. After performance reached a certain level of Reliability, AI Systems became viable for Integration into High-Stakes Environments.

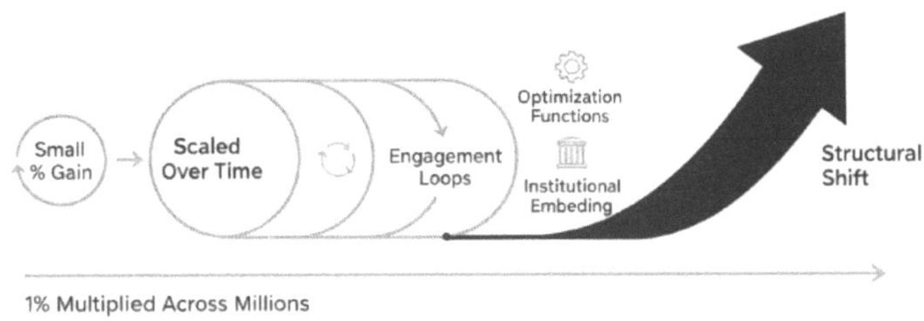

AI Systems were integrated into Credit Scoring Pipelines by Financial Institutions. Hospitals implemented Predictive Analytics for Readmission Risk. Retail Platforms were using Real-Time Recommendation Engines Optimized for Conversion.

Law Enforcement Agencies were experimenting with Risk Assessment Tools. At this point, the Defining Question changed from "Is the Model Accurate?" to "What Objective is Being Optimized at Scale?" Optimization Functions Are Not Neutral Mathematical Abstractions. Optimization Functions Encode Institutional Priorities.

If a Recommendation System Is Optimizing for Engagement Time, it is Elevating Content that Provokes Interaction. If a Logistics Platform Is Optimizing for Delivery Speed, it May Be Deprioritizing Environmental Cost. If a Hiring Algorithm Is Optimizing for Historical Performance

Indicators, it Risks Reinforcing Existing Demographic Patterns Embedded in Prior Hiring Data. Over time, these Optimization Choices accumulate. They Shape Markets, Behaviors, and Expectations. A One-Percent Improvement in Engagement May Appear Marginal in Quarterly Reporting. Multiplied Across Hundreds of Millions of Users Over a Decade, It Reshapes Attention Economies and Media Ecosystems.

INSTITUTIONAL DEPENDENCY AND THE RECONFIGURATION OF EXPERTISE

A trend across many industries has emerged: as AI becomes more reliable, so too does institutional dependency increase. In trading markets, for example, computer algorithms complete the vast majority of high-frequency trades today. What was once a role of making trades has now evolved to monitoring/controlling systems created by others. In radiology, diagnostic models are used to assist in interpreting images and flag abnormalities with very high sensitivity. Supply chain management uses predictive AI to forecast product demand months in advance.

These changes deliver quantifiable benefits, including reduced errors, increased efficiency, and lower operational costs. Some pilot studies have shown that AI-assisted workflows produce productivity gains of 15-30% across specific task categories.

However, another dynamic associated with AI integration rarely appears on organizations' performance dashboards: the changing nature of human expertise. Over time, as systems produce consistent recommendations, professional experts must adjust how they use their cognitive abilities.

Eventually, tasks that were once viewed as core competencies can transition to oversight-type roles. Younger or entry-level employees, who traditionally develop expertise through repetition and correction, may now be relying on an AI-generated draft. The pathway to developing expertise changes slightly. This does not mean that there will always be a decline in human expertise. Rather, it means that there will be a structural change.

Therefore, if an organization becomes heavily dependent on automated decision support systems, its ability to recover from the systems' failure will depend on whether it has preserved human capacity to function in their absence. Aviation serves as a cautionary example of this. Autopilot systems have significantly improved the safety of commercial air travel. Aviation researchers have identified cases in which excessive reliance on autopilot systems has degraded manual flying skills and created a new risk in the event of an unanticipated disengagement. The same phenomenon applies to the broad adoption of AI. The legacy of AI will not only reflect the kinds of things machines will learn to do, but also the kinds of things humans will gradually stop practicing.

FEEDBACK LOOPS AT SOCIETAL SCALE

One of the most underestimated capabilities of AI systems is their ability to create cycles of feedback spanning years rather than days.

For example, predictive policing algorithms, which determine where to deploy patrol resources based on historical incident data, can lead to more incidents by providing greater opportunities for law enforcement observation in a neighborhood with a history of crime. Those newly created incidents will be included in the model as data and will provide evidence that the original allocation was correct.

Similarly, recommendation engine algorithms on digital platforms do not simply reflect user preferences but also influence exposure patterns, thereby shaping user preferences over time. Content ranking models trained on metrics such as engagement tend to amplify material that elicits an emotional response. The emotional response drives user interaction, and that interaction reinforces the ranking of that material over extended periods. This process has been known to drive political polarization, cultural narratives, and trust in information ecosystems over the years. These phenomena are not speculative but have been observed as consequences of optimization at scale.

The primary difference between artificial intelligence and previous information technologies is its adaptability. The system does not follow fixed rules; it adjusts parameters based on how users interact with it. This creates dynamic cycles of feedback in which the model shapes user behavior, which in turn shapes subsequent behavior. Legacy in this context is emergent; it is generated through interactions among millions of individuals and algorithmic adjustments over extended time horizons.

GOVERNANCE AS THE DETERMINANT OF HISTORICAL JUDGMENT

Historical patterns show that technology has a double standard: technological capabilities can both make or break a society; additionally, how a society chooses to manage these capabilities can ultimately determine its success. Mechanized industrial production raised productivity at an incredible rate. Still, it was not until there were regulations in place to prevent labor exploitation and environmental damage that we could begin to see the benefits of this type of production. Similarly, nuclear physics provided us with unprecedented levels of energy; however, the same energy source that has enabled our modern world has also led to non-proliferation treaties and deterrence doctrines to keep the threat of weapons out of the hands of rogue nations and terrorist organizations. AI will likely follow a similar pattern of development.

Future historians will not simply look back at the history of AI to identify who first deployed the most sophisticated model, nor will they look at who first developed the best AI model. They will instead analyze when the first audit mechanism was implemented to detect and correct systemic biases in the models. They will assess if companies deployed AI quickly enough to establish clear transparency standards. And, they will evaluate if the government maintained oversight authority over AI systems that affect the economy (credit, employment), healthcare, and justice (criminal justice). Already, some governments have begun including Algorithmic Impact Assessments (AIA) in their public procurement processes. Documenting AI models using model cards and documenting the systems themselves using System Reports have become the norm in Responsible AI practices. More and more independent Oversight Boards and Red-Team Exercises are being implemented in the development of AI systems.

At this time, these practices may seem like minor bureaucratic steps, but historically they will be seen as significant milestones. If future generations see that the ability to develop capable AI systems develops alongside governance and regulation, then the history of AI may be told as a story about how a new technology helped stabilize the effectiveness of governmental agencies. On the other hand, if the development of capable AI systems far outpaces adequate governance and regulation, then the history of AI may be a story of cycles of public backlash, regulatory overcorrection, and distrust of government and technology.

The course of history is still open.

INTERGENERATIONAL CONSEQUENCES

The most significant way legacy manifests is through intergenerational normalization. Children entering elementary school today will be working with artificial intelligence (AI)-driven tutoring systems, AI-driven recommendation engines, and AI-driven voice assistants. The university student of today is drafting essays with significant help from AI. Young professionals are entering work environments where predictive dashboards are used to make many strategic business decisions. As such, for young people today, AI will not be an innovative technology, it will be their normal environment.

Younger people will not discuss whether they agree or disagree with the idea of using algorithms to filter information; they will assume that filtering is a fundamental part of accessing information on the Internet. Younger people will not question if hiring systems use predictive analytics; they will assume that they do.

Younger people will likely not see personalization as optional, but rather as the norm. The norms established by younger people today regarding what they consider acceptable levels of privacy, agency, and authority will directly influence how younger people think about the role of government and institutions in the future. Legacy is often invisible when it is developed. However, it is often not until there are limited alternatives available that the existence of legacy becomes apparent.

INCENTIVES AS THE HIDDEN ARCHITECT

Artificial intelligence amplifies the incentives embedded within its development ecosystem. If venture capital prioritizes aggressive growth and rapid scaling, models will be deployed quickly, sometimes before long-term consequences are fully understood. If public funding emphasizes equitable access and societal benefit, research priorities may shift accordingly. If consumers reward convenience over privacy safeguards, design choices will reflect that demand.

In high-level strategy discussions, trade-offs are frequently framed in technical language: interpretability versus performance, robustness versus speed, personalization versus privacy. Beneath those technical trade-offs lie normative judgments about what kind of society is being optimized.

- Do we privilege efficiency over deliberation? Do we prioritize market advantage over collective stability?
  Do we treat AI as proprietary leverage or shared infrastructure?

Whether AI distributes capabilities or consolidates power will depend on the answers to these questions.

THE MEASURE OF OUR INTELLIGENCE

The title of this book is not accidental.

The intelligence we built is not an external force. It is an extension of institutional design, economic incentive, and human ambition. It reflects our capacity for abstraction and pattern recognition. It also reflects our blind spots and structural biases. The legacy of artificial intelligence will not ultimately be measured in parameter counts or benchmark scores. It will be measured in institutional resilience, distributive fairness, epistemic stability, and public trust.

- It will be measured by whether societies strengthen human judgment while augmenting it with machine prediction.
- It will be measured by whether accountability mechanisms evolved alongside capability.
- It will be measured by whether intelligence at scale empowered citizens or concentrated authority.

The systems we build today will become tomorrow's default assumptions. The optimization objectives selected this decade will influence social and economic patterns for generations. Unlike software bugs, structural legacies cannot be patched easily after normalization. They require foresight at the moment of integration.

Artificial intelligence is more than just a new technology. The organization, distribution, and governance of intellect itself are matters of civilizational choice. The systems we normalize will be passed down to future generations. The enduring question is whether they will regard that inheritance as an expansion of possibility. or as a constraint shaped by short-term vision.

That judgment will define the legacy of our intelligence.

CONCLUSION

When I began working closely with artificial intelligence systems, the dominant concern in most institutions was their technological feasibility. Can models grow to scale? Will the models' performance remain steady and accurate in real-world situations? Are the data pipelines robust and reliable enough to maintain the deployments?

As it eventually emerged, however, these are just the first set of questions. Once AI systems move beyond experimental tools and become embedded in production and operational environments, the next, more critical adjustment occurs. As AI systems perform their functions and complete tasks more quickly and with greater precision, the way decisions are made, justified, and distributed within organizations changes.

Predictive models in financial services have evolved from being analytical aid tools to becoming fundamental building blocks of risk assessments. Diagnostic models in healthcare went from experimental research tools to clinical tools that influence patient treatment paths. Automated forecasting models in corporate settings started to shape the strategic planning cycles. Each deployment was rational and supported by tangible increases in both efficiency and accuracy. However, each deployment also represented a subtle transfer of authority to systems capable of statistical prediction.

Human judgment did not go away; it simply rearranged itself around model-based output. More and more professionals were evaluating the probability outputs of models instead of developing their own independent probability constructs. In many cases, oversight took over the origination function. This reorganization is not inherently destructive, but it is a fundamental change in how expertise is expressed.

One of the most consistent lessons I have seen is that artificial intelligence systems amplify the current organizational incentives with incredible speed and efficiency. Whether the organization is focused on rapid growth, the AI system will optimize for it unrelentingly. When historical data sets contain embedded inequalities, predictive systems will reproduce those inequalities with mathematical consistency. Where governance mechanisms are weak, deployment will proceed faster than accountability can keep pace.

AI systems do not have an inherent moral direction. Institutional context does. While the AI is often characterized as a significant increase in capability, it also has the potential to be a radical transformation of institutional design. For hundreds of years, authority to make decisions rested on accumulated human experience.

The AI introduces predictive systems that can synthesize large-scale patterns that no single individual can analyze. By integrating these systems into organizations' decision-making processes, this fundamentally transforms the epistemological base of the organizations. This transformation requires discipline. The predictive accuracy of a model does not equate to moral authority. The statistical confidence of a model does not remove uncertainty. While automating processes can reduce friction, it cannot reduce the responsibility associated with those processes.

Our legacy will not be measured by the benchmark performance of the AI systems nor by their ability to compute complex calculations. Our legacy will be determined by whether we develop accountable practices at the same pace as we develop capabilities. If AI systems are designed to operate as open, transparent, and governed systems, then they have the potential to strengthen institutions and expand human capacity. However, if AI systems are deployed and operated without sufficient governance, the potential exists for the concentration of authority that is difficult to reverse. The systems that we develop today will be the default position of tomorrow. Changing the default position is much more difficult than debating the proposal. Therefore, the current moment presents issues that transcend the normal scope of quarterly performance measurements and competing positions.

The destiny of the AI systems is not predetermined. It is a matter of structured choice operating at scale. How seriously we take the choices we are making will determine whether the intelligence we have created becomes a stabilizing force within our societies or creates a new level of structural fragility. Our history will not judge us based on what we accomplished technologically. We will be judged by whether we balanced the intelligence we developed with the corresponding degree of responsibility.

BIBLIOGRAPHY

- Bostrom, Nick. *Superintelligence: Paths, Dangers, Strategies.* Oxford: Oxford University Press, 2014.
- Russell, Stuart. *Human Compatible: Artificial Intelligence and the Problem of Control.* New York: Viking, 2019.
- Tegmark, Max. *Life 3.0: Being Human in the Age of Artificial Intelligence.* New York: Knopf, 2017.
- Brynjolfsson, Erik, and Andrew McAfee. *The Second Machine Age: Work, Progress, and Prosperity in a Time of Brilliant Technologies.* New York: W. W. Norton, 2014.
- Brynjolfsson, Erik, and Andrew McAfee. *Machine, Platform, Crowd: Harnessing Our Digital Future.* New York: W. W. Norton, 2017.
- Zuboff, Shoshana. *The Age of Surveillance Capitalism.* New York: PublicAffairs, 2019.
- O'Neil, Cathy. *Weapons of Math Destruction: How Big Data Increases Inequality and Threatens Democracy.* New York: Crown, 2016.
- Kahneman, Daniel. *Thinking, Fast and Slow.* New York: Farrar, Straus and Giroux, 2011.
- Domingos, Pedro. *The Master Algorithm: How the Quest for the Ultimate Learning Machine Will Remake Our World.* New York: Basic Books, 2015.

- Goodfellow, Ian, Yoshua Bengio, and Aaron Courville. *Deep Learning.* Cambridge, MA: MIT Press, 2016.
- Mitchell, Melanie. *Artificial Intelligence: A Guide for Thinking Humans.* New York: Farrar, Straus and Giroux, 2019.
- Floridi, Luciano. *The Ethics of Information.* Oxford: Oxford University Press, 2013.
- Floridi, Luciano. *The Fourth Revolution: How the Infosphere Is Reshaping Human Reality.* Oxford: Oxford University Press, 2014.
- Acemoglu, Daron, and Simon Johnson. *Power and Progress: Our Thousand-Year Struggle Over Technology and Prosperity.* New York: PublicAffairs, 2023.
- Acemoglu, Daron, and James A. Robinson. *Why Nations Fail: The Origins of Power, Prosperity, and Poverty.* New York: Crown, 2012.
- Harari, Yuval Noah. *Homo Deus: A Brief History of Tomorrow.* New York: Harper, 2017.
- Harari, Yuval Noah. *21 Lessons for the 21st Century.* New York: Spiegel & Grau, 2018.
- Kearns, Michael, and Aaron Roth. *The Ethical Algorithm: The Science of Socially Aware Algorithm Design.* Oxford: Oxford University Press, 2019.

- Susskind, Richard. *Tomorrow's Lawyers: An Introduction to Your Future.* Oxford: Oxford University Press, 2017.
- Susskind, Daniel. *A World Without Work: Technology, Automation, and How We Should Respond.* New York: Metropolitan Books, 2020.

www.ingramcontent.com/pod-product-compliance
Lightning Source LLC
LaVergne TN
LVHW051129210926
848482LV00001B/34